Foreword

Nostalgic Preston is a compilation of photographs and interesting facts from the past. In producing this book, the publishers had a very simple aim; to use the pages here as a catalyst, to bring back memories of what the area used to be like not so-long-ago, a time within the memory of most local folk. Nostalgic Preston is not intended to be a history book - it has more to do with entertainment than serious study - but if the book prompts people with an interest in their area to go out and buy one or two of the excellent local history books available, then so much the better.

Preston has undergone many changes in the last 50 years and, compared to some other northern towns and cities, has come out of the experience in better shape than most. People will look back at the passing of some of the fine old buildings which once graced the area - such as the old Town Hall - but should rejoice in the preservation of others, like the Harris Museum, Library and Art Gallery, and the Miller Arcade, which have stood the test of time despite one or two close-shaves! Local industry has shaped the character of the town and trends in retail architecture and design have influenced the appearance of the town centre. Many of the pictures were chosen because they reflect these important changes. Nostalgic Preston has been a pleasure to compile - I do hope you enjoy reading it.

Phil Holland

A Lightning over the Ribble, with Preston in the distance.

Published in November 1996 by:
True North Publishing,
Dean Clough Industrial Park,
Halifax. HX3 5AX. Telephone 01422 344344
Repro. by Transgraphic Ltd., Morley.
Printed by Joseph Ward ColourPrint Ltd., Dewsbury.

true north
PUBLISHING

£4.99
(Nett)

Contents

Acknowledgments

Many people and organisations have made the production of this modest book possible and deserve thanks here. The British Aerospace North West Heritage Group provided many previously unpublished photographs which are certain to rekindle memories of the marvellous work that has been carried on there over the years. Thanks too must go to Colin Charnley of British Aerospace for his invaluable input. The Harris Museum and Art Gallery supplied many of the photographs used from their extensive collection and we are pleased to acknowledge their assistance. Peter Reed is a local photographer who has supplied photographs to the national press for many years. We are grateful to him for supplying several excellent photographs contained within these pages. Finally, thank you to the advertisers who are featured here - for their interesting archive material and support which helped us keep the price of the book to a reasonable level, and to Gareth Martin who co-ordinated the advertising content.

Memories from the archives of British Aerospace...

The following pages in this section are devoted to an organisation which has touched the lives of thousands of people from Preston and the surrounding area for over 100 years. British Aerospace, as it is now known, has played a key role, not only in the history of Preston, but in the defence and commercial success of the country as a whole. We are indebted to the *unsung heroes* of the British Aerospace North West Heritage Group - an enthusiastic team of past and present employees of the company, who are tasked with the job of maintaining the archives and history of the organisation. Their help was been invaluable to the publishers.
Pictured above are four different Marks of Canberra at the Warton Aerodrome.

Left: The Strand Road East Works seen in this view at the turn of the century, was then the site of the electric carriage works and is now demolished. The open land in the foreground is today occupied by G.E.C. *Below:* In a different view of the works, the tower housing the clock and bell can be seen. This was later demolished and the gap bridged to form a new entrance gate. *Below, left:* A well known product was tramcars and these can still be seen in Blackpool. This scale model was built by apprentices for the 1902 *Guild.*

Strand Road remembered

Right: The Strand Road Experiment and Design works after its completion in September 1940. It was still known as *Vineys*.

Below: An exterior view of Viney's Haulage Company which was demolished for the new aircraft offices and erection shop (seen in the photograph on the right) in 1939.

Below, right: A steam wagon and trailer operated by H. Viney and Co. Ltd., complete with solid tyres, seen here in the early years of this century.

The development of Strand Road

Right: The Strand Road machine shop, seen here in 1941, when wartime production of aircraft components for a variety of aircraft was in full swing.

Above: This breathtaking view of the front sections of Halifax bombers was captured in October 1943 in the Viney's area of Strand Road. The sheer scale of production is difficult for us to imagine today, and the success that the company and it's workforce achieved in producing these aircraft was a significant element of the overall war effort. 2,145 Halifax bombers were constructed in Preston. Completed Halifax and Hampden bombers were flown from Samlesbury airfield.

Above, right: The English Electric connection is well known. Originally part of the Dick, Kerr's company, the firm had many interests - including the production of locomotives - and a huge engine for one can be seen here.

Below: During the Second World War the West Works had been engaged in the manufacture of equipment to support the war effort. At the end of the war production reverted to railway locomotives and domestic appliances. One of the most famous products ever to leave this English Electric site was the locomotive pictured below. The Deltic - seen here in prototype form in about 1955, won many orders for the company as well as the hearts of many diesel locomotive enthusiasts. The locomotive soon became the backbone of British Railways' London Kings Cross to Edinburgh main line service.

Above: Another view of the West Works after the war, probably in the 1950s - showing rolling stock under construction for the foreign market. This was an important activity for English Electric at the time.

THE **ENGLISH ELECTRIC** CO. LTD

Aviation memories: Warton aerodrome remembered.....

Work first began on the Warton Aerodrome site around 1940. Initially five aircraft hangars were built and R.A.F personnel became based here from 1941. Further major work, by the MacAlpine construction company, was carried out in 1942. The following year saw the arrival of the American Airforce and the establishment of the facility as "Base Air Depot No.2". At its peak, there were 20,000 American service personnel operating from the base. As the war drew to a close the Technical Training School enabled servicemen to be re-educated ready for their return to civilian life. At this time too, there was a large number of German prisoners of war on the site providing many labour services.

During its active period as Base Air Depot No.2, from July 1943 to the latter part of 1945, the 20,000 servicemen on the site were employed in a variety of technical trades. Their principal function was to receive new aircraft from the U.S.A and incorporate in them certain modifications to fit them for operational use, before delivery to the various American Air Force Stations in the U.K.

This was a time of intense activity at Warton. There would be up to 3,000 aircraft parked at the site awaiting their turn to be worked on in the hangars. Bombers were parked side by side along both sides of the runways and perimeter tracks, with smaller fighters parked underneath their wings. Only the main (2608) runway was kept clear for incoming and outgoing flights. A fleet of 1500 vehicles was used to transport people, parts and tools around the busy base. In order to upgrade the perimeter tracks to take the weight of the heavy bombers, a team of 800 U.S

servicemen from a special construction corps were drafted in. They completed the work in six months.

After the War......

The first small party of staff from *English Electric*, from the 45 or so aircraft designers based in Preston, arrived at Warton in 1947. In 1948 the first main party of just over 100 people arrived in preparation for the final assembly of the first Canberra. At this time several hangars were still occupied by the R.A.F's maintenance unit.

In 1949 the first Canberra prototype flew from Warton and in 1950 most of the design and technical staff moved there from Preston. The flight of the P.1B prototype Lightning in April 1957 was an important milestone in the history of the company. In the same year the newly extended runway was joined by a new control tower and further improvements took place to the runway and support systems, including high speed wind tunnels, over the next decade. By the mid 1960s the design staff numbered almost 4,000 and 10,000 Lightning test flights had been made. Today, Warton still plays a key role in the prestigious British Aerospace organisation.

Warton, winter 1959: English Electric P.1 (Lightning) pre-production batch. (L-R) Desmond De Villiers, Peter Hillwood, Jimmy Dell, and Roland Beamont

Lightning over the Ribble with Preston in the distance

This Halifax bomber - a B11 Series 1 (Special) with Defiant type dorsal turret - was delivered between 31 March and 13 April 1943 by English Electric to 78 Squadron of 4 Group, Bomber Command, at Breighton, Yorkshire. It failed to return from a raid on Gelsenkirchen, just two months after this picture was taken at Samlesbury.

Samlesbury, the early years.......

The Samlesbury site of British Aerospace Military Aircraft lies partly in South Ribble, and the origins of the airfield go back to 1922, when it was first proposed to serve Blackburn and Preston. In April 1939 the Air Ministry instructed the English Electric Company to proceed with the construction of Flight Shed No.1 on the proposed site of the municipal aerodrome, to enable the aircraft which were being produced at the Preston and Rugby works to be tested in flight. The first Hampden bomber, constructed at the Preston works, made its first flight from Samlesbury on February 22 1940. By December 1942, five hangars and three runways had been built at Samlesbury, and a total of 770 Hampdens and 2145 Halifax bombers were delivered from the

base during the remainder of the Second World War. In 1945, in accordance with Government policy of the time, English Electric formed an aircraft division to design and develop military aircraft. In 1947 the company took over Warton Aerodrome. The first aircraft designed and built by English Electric was the Canberra, in 1949. In 1960, English Electric Aviation was incorporated into the British Aircraft Corporation (BAC) and, in 1964, was re-named the Preston Division of BAC. In 1971 it became the Military Aircraft Division and, in 1977 when BAC was absorbed into the newly created British Aerospace, the Warton, Preston and Samlesbury sites came together to form the Warton Division. In 1989 the company became a subsidiary company of British Aerospace Plc and was re-named British Aerospace Military Aircraft Ltd.

The earliest *local* origins of the organisation now known as British Aerospace can be traced back to the company created by two shrewd Scots engineers - W.B. Dick and John Kerr. Dick, Kerr's - as the company was known - built railway rolling stock at the East Works along Strand Road from 1897. Early success and expansion resulted in the building of the West Works in 1900 on land which had been reclaimed as a result of the diverting of the river Ribble. The company manufactured many products, including seaplanes, munitions, lightbulbs, electric trams, domestic appliances, locomotives - including the famous diesel *Deltic,* and later, aircraft. The Dick, Kerr ladies football team, pictured here, was as famous in Preston as some of the company's products were throughout the rest of world.

Final assembly of Canberra aircraft before production flight from Samlesbury. The aircraft first flew in 1949 - and many were still in service 40 years later.

Shopping spree.......

Below: One of the first self-service supermarkets in Preston is pictured below, in this photograph from 1964. It was situated at Ribbleton Lane

Above: Curiosity greeted the opening of Britain's first Kentucky Fried Chicken shop on a Preston high street. The year was 1965 and the window proclaimed the opening offer of chicken and chips for two shillings (10p). Less than good news for the staff at the Wimpy next door if the prices in their window are anything to go by.

The fascinating story behind E.H. Booth & Co. Ltd

Edwin Henry Booth was born in Bury in the early 19th century. He was the son of a Doctor Booth who died suddenly while Edwin was still young. His mother then remarried a widower whom Edwin described as creating "hell on earth" in their home. His stepfather turned out to be a drunkard and fraudulent businessman who, through his malpractices, was forced to flee the country with Edwin's mother for a while.

The Founder's first job

From the age of ten, Edwin would often walk to seek refuge with friends as far afield as Manchester and Bolton, and, upon returning home from time to time, would find himself most unwelcome. Eventually, he ran away from home for good and found employ-

Mr E.H. Booth

ment as a Tailor's errand boy.

Over the ensuing years, Edwin endured much hardship, and only his overwhelming belief in providence gave him the strength and endurance to improve his lot. At the age of fifteen he gained a position with a grocer in Preston and, through night school and studying late into the evening, sought to make up for his lack of education in previous years.

The tea trade

At the age of nineteen his employer sent him to Liverpool to learn about the tea trade, with the idea that upon his return they could open a store in Blackpool. At this time the resort was just emerging as a popular holiday resort as a consequence of the newly opened rail link with Preston. Things did not work out as planned however, as Edwin's employer was not in a position to extend his business after all and Edwin was informed that he was free to leave.

"Booths" is born....

Having visited Blackpool and realised the potential to sell groceries, Edwin persuaded his old employer to lend him £80.00 worth of stock. Having already identified premises for which he agreed to pay a rental of £15.00 per annum, he then paid £20.00 to make the necessary alterations and, after 3 months trading, succeeded in making a profit of £50.00 after paying expenses. "Booths" was born.

Seven years later in 1885, Edwin opened his first branch in Chorley and recorded that a horse and "gig" were bought for £28.00! The original Preston store was opened in the market place in 1859 and it was not until 1867 that the Preston business was

moved to Fishergate, where the Head Office has been situated to this day.

There have been many highlights along the way for Booths over the years, few being more significant than the staff bonus scheme in 1909. This scheme was the forerunner of the profit-related pay scheme that is in place today. Later, in 1920 "Mr John" was to offer shares in the company to employees for the first time. In 1947 "Mr Kenny" wrote of the founder that "he was intensely proud of the business he had built up and stated that he sold the best goods he could buy in shops staffed with first class assistants". Today the "mission statement" remains unchanged because everyone in the company knows that the customer's expectations must always be met at the highest possible level.

E H BOOTH
&COMPANY
LTD

Above, left: The Penwortham shop as it was in 1937.

Above: Booth's Fishergate store seen here around 1910.

Top right: A promotional teapot depicting the Boot's store situated at 20, Market Place from 1859.

Right: The interior of Booth's Fishergate in the 1930s.

Above: A 1960s shopping scene captured in Preston. The rise of the car and concrete era resulted in many changes to traditional shopping habits. Multi-decked shopping malls with adjacent acres of car parking space started to appear in every town from the early 1960s. Thankfully, Preston did better than most in terms of the retention of traditional shopping areas and the standard of architecture achieved in the new ones.

Right: Crystal House was never the most popular building in Preston. It was constructed in 1964 - on the site of the old Town Hall which had served the town from 1782 to 1862- and not to be confused with the later building which was built in 1867 and destroyed by fire in 1947.

Below: The corner of Chapel Street on Fishergate - complete with two-way motor traffic of course, in this photograph from the mid 1950s.

They don't make shops like this anymore. The Fishergate premises of J. Heaney's Fish, Game and Fruit Dealer, with the proprietor, J.E. Gardner standing proudly under the canopy and surrounded by a variety of dead animals. The picture was taken in 1902.

Whittles - family jewellers since 1860

The popular family jewellery business known as Whittles was started in about 1860. At the time it was one of the first retail businesses to occupy the Fishergate area and was then situated further along the road where *Boots* the chemists are at the present time. The opening of the Miller Arcade in 1901 was to dramatically change shopping habits in Preston at the turn of the century, and Whittles saw their future in this part of town. The move to the Miller Arcade, after 40 years on Fishergate came soon after it opened, and *Whittles* remained there until 1967.

Change of ownership.

1932 saw a change of ownership for Preston's best known jewellers. James Rhodes was the grandfather of the present managing director. A successful businessman in his own right, he had two sons and wished to see each of them set up in their own business. He bought the firm for his son Roland.

Thus it was that Roland Rhodes took on the task of developing the already sound jewellery business in the Miller Arcade.

At the time the business passed into the ownership of the Rhodes family it was appointed the agency for Rolex watches - the most prestigious watch manufacturer in the world. This association has lasted until this day - a span of over 60 years.

Return to Fishergate.

In 1967 the lease expired in the Miller Arcade and it was decided that the interests of the business would be best served by a move to a new location. Fishergate, the original base of *Whittles* had always had a special place in the affections of the Rhodes family, and it was decided to relocate to this popular part of Preston. The premises acquired at the time were situated at 111 Fishergate, next to the Halifax Building Society offices. 21 years later the firm moved again, to its present location at 47 Fishergate, right at the heart of retailing activity.

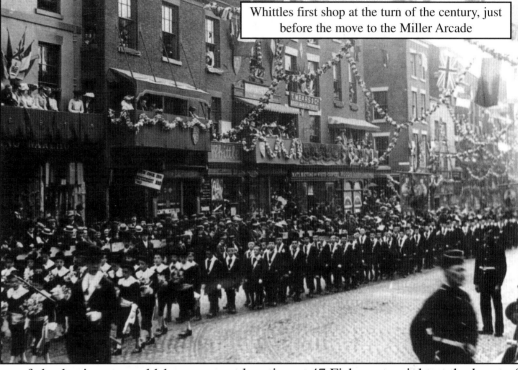

Whittles first shop at the turn of the century, just before the move to the Miller Arcade

In addition to a very strong watch business, supported by excellent workshop facilities, is a fine diamond/coloured stone ring jewellery service which centres around stones bought from companies all over the world. The designs of these magnificent pieces are as distinctive as the company itself.

The current MD, Mr Brian Rhodes has completed 38 years service with the company - and he confidently expects to serve many more still - in between rounds of golf, his *other* passion in life. Brian Rhodes is proud of his staff, some of whom have been with the firm for 30 years, and proud of the service *Whittles* has given to Preston for over 130 years.

James Hall - the inspiration for a North-West retailing dynasty.

James Hall, founder of James Hall & Co., moved to Southport from Roseacre after his marriage in 1863, when he started a provisions business, curing bacon and baking bread.

The business prospered, but the chain of supply needed improvement, so he started to supply other shops with his products. This led to his interest in wholesaling. He wanted to enable retailers to provide good food at reasonable prices in the communities in which they traded. His principle is still fundamental to the company's policy. As business in wholesaling grew, so did the need for larger premises, and before the founder's death in 1901 four moves to larger premises, all in Southport, had taken place.

Nine Children

Five of James Hall's nine children entered the business, and during the period between 1901 and the end of the First World War the range of goods han-

dled had increased, more transportation was required and extra premises in Nelson Street, Preston were acquired. In 1928 a serious fire necessitated the rebuilding of the Southport premises and in 1935, a Preston Company, R. Bannister & Co. Ltd., were purchased and the company operated the former Bannister's premises, situated along Heatley Street in Preston as an additional distribution point. The brothers and sisters of the Hall family worked successfully together for over 50 years, continually adopting modern methods. At the end of the 1939-45 war a third generation of directors, Stuart, Stanley and Philip Hall assumed control.

The introduction of SPAR.

In 1956, with five other leading progressive wholesalers, the company was instrumental in introducing Spar to the U.K. This coincided with the building of a new warehouse in Preston, followed by the conversion of the old depot into one of the first wholesale Frozen Food depots in the country.

The next ten years saw tremendous growth in the company, due to the combination of the introduction of Spar and the improved road systems in the area allowing wholesaling activities to extend to the present franchise area.

In 1966, the present premises on Blackpool Road Preston were acquired to allow the whole operation to be carried out from one Centre, and in the late 70s Ian and Andrew Hall became the fourth generation of the Hall family to be appointed directors of the com-

pany. In 1977, Ian Hall became managing director, and in 1986 Andrew Hall and Ian Hall became joint managing directors. Progress has led to expansion

requiring the building of new warehouses for Grocery, Frozen Foods and Fresh Foods totalling over 8,000 sq.m of additional space.

The company now serves over 360 Spar outlets within an area which extends from North Wales to the Humber in the South, and up to the Scottish Borders in the North.

The company has always placed all its resources behind the development of the Spar concept in the U.K. The convenience concept, Spar shops trading longer hours and open seven days a week, was adopted by Spar in the 80s. The major grocers were quite content with the sales and profits their large scale supermarkets could achieve, and most of Spar's more direct competitors were lagging behind. 8 Till Late catapulted Spar to the forefront of convenience shop-

and Company, there has been continuous investment in the development of the independent retail sector, and Spar members have been at the forefront of this investment. A typical Spar shop in the North of England will now offer long opening hours, in some instances 24 hours a day, and a combination of Groceries, Newspapers, Beers, Wines and Spirits, Cigarettes, Snacks, Confectionery and Hot and Fresh Foods. With modern technology and, in particular, the advancement of computer facilities available, not only to the wholesale operation, but also to the retail operation, James Hall and Company and Spar have made significant developments in past few years. With the development of the convenience store concept still in its relative infancy, as far as the U.K is concerned, the company will continue to progress and develop the Spar business throughout the North of England.

ping, with longer opening hours, improved store standards and range enhancement. All around Britain, independent retailers and wholesalers prospered with Spar.

Competition.
Today, the picture is different. Everyone recognised the importance of convenience in the eyes of the consumer, the multiples open late and sell petrol, and the petrol companies sell groceries 24 hours a day. Nowadays, the consumer can usually choose between a number of suitable local outlets and James Hall and Company with Spar, has a single objective, to have them think of Spar as the best local shopping option.

Commitment to retailing.....
Throughout the history of James Hall

Modern Times.
From its very modest beginnings the business has grown into a major force in the world of retailing serving over 360 Spar stores in the North of England. The founder of the company, James Hall, is never far from the thoughts of current family members who play an active part in the running of the business. They can only wonder of what he would make of the way the business he began has grown and flourished since he created it over 130 years ago.

Left: Dramatic scenes along Church Street in March 1965. Fire had broken out at Gooby's store bringing this busy part of Preston to a complete standstill. Crowds of onlookers are seen here as firemen struggle to contain the blaze and prevent it from spreading to adjacent shops.

Right: Few Preston folk over the age of 20 will fail to remember the major fire at Preston Farmers which ravaged the building on the night of February 11 1970. Crowds of anxious residents from the surrounding streets were forced out of doors by the scale and intensity of the blaze. This thought-provoking scene was captured by Peter Reed at 2.00am on the night in question.

Far right: October 10 1968 saw this major fire at the premises of Northern Ireland Trailers on Preston Dock. The billowing smoke could be seen over 20 miles away.

999-Emergency!

Z-Cars

The TV series "Z-Cars" broke new ground in the field of television police drama in the 1960s. Broadcast live, it attracted a huge following and the star cast, including *Barlow, Watt, Lynch* and *"Fancy" Smith* went on to become household names. They are seen here on a visit to County Police Headquarters in May 1964.

Right: "Hold this picture two inches from your nose and move it backwards slowly, while leaving your eyes totally relaxed...." Only kidding, the picture records the first delivery of *Panda Cars* to local Police in May 1967 - not one of those optical illusions made popular by some of the Sunday papers. Pandas were popular with forces throughout the country and seen as the modern way of achieving quick response and high profile policing. Their popularity lasted less than 30 years.

Tithe Barn Street Fire Station. The precise date when this photograph was taken is not known, but it is thought to have been in the 1930s. This fine old building had been enlarged in 1905, as can be seen from the lettering above the first archway. After many years of faithful service, and much to the regret of many local people who had benefited from the efforts of the brave men based here, the station was demolished in the 1960s.

Preston Guilds past

Preston Guild

Above: A view from 1952 sees the town elaborately decorated for the Preston Guild of that year. Note the tower of the Fishergate Baptist Church (built in 1857) peeping out over the banner in the centre of the photograph.

Left: An atmospheric scene from the 1902 Preston Guild. On the left of the picture the Miller Arcade can just be made out - note the distinctive roof work on the corner tower. At this time the Miller Arcade had been open for just 4 years.

Below: This 1902 photograph shows Flagmarket in a scene captured to record the celebrations for that year's Preston Guild. In the distance Friargate can be seen with the start of Market Street visible on the right of the picture. The area on the right of the photograph had been the subject of considerable redevelopment in the early 1890s which involved the widening of Friargate.

Above: This lovely photograph depicts a charming scene from the 1952 Preston Guild. It shows one of the dozens of floats which were carefully and lovingly prepared by local enthusiasts for the procession.

This flat-backed truck carried the slogan Hawkins Treasures and had a *safety-first* theme. It was complete with nursery rhymes and characters portrayed by local children, no doubt it warmly applauded by the spectators.

Left: A lovely picture from the Preston Guild in 1952 which really captures the atmosphere of the occasion *and* the beginning of the 'fifties. The photograph is interesting for a number of reasons, not least of which being the banner being proudly held aloft which appears to represent the church which stands behind it. The building in question is believed to be the Wesleyan Church at Fulwood. Many people will have fond memories of day trips to the coast or the Lakes on coaches such as the ones pictured here. Coach excursions had always been popular, but post-war Britain saw a boom in the availability and enjoyment of trips and holidays among ordinary working people.

Above: Another float in the 1952 Preston Guild, this one having a nautical theme and travelling past a seated area on the route of the procession.

Left: The 1952 Guild again, but this photograph is included here for the rare view of the Theatre Royal which, at the time, was showing the popular production *Ivanhoe*.

Preston
Guild

Street party

Two scenes from a street party held during the Preston Guild celebrations in 1972. The location is Miles Street. Children have been an important element of Guild celebrations ever since 1842 when they were organised to sing together on the Market Place.

The Children's Pageant of 1922 marked the time when the participation of children in the Guilds became a regular and organised feature of the celebrations. This was repeated in the Guilds of 1952, 1972 and 1992.

Avenham Park as it is rarely seen, in a picture taken by Peter Reed from the platform of an Army helicopter. The photograph shows the intriguing symmetry of the stage and display area for the Children's Pageant in the 1972 Guild.

Left: "Work for Victory" was the message in this photograph of staff at Gregson and Monks (Loom Manufacturers) dating from about 1942. Like so many Preston companies, Gregson and Monks found themselves very much involved in supporting the war effort in the years between 1939 and 1945.

Production of looms was suspended and countless thousands of shells were produced instead by the willing workforce.

Below: The installation of a massive new engine to power the growing business of J.R and A. Smith (Velvet Weavers) at Manchester Mill was reason enough to take this staff photograph at the time. The mill was situated at Mosely Street, off New Hall Lane, and the date shown on the back of the photograph is 1922.

Working life in Preston.....

Left: A 1940s photograph of the Training Centre at Greenbank Mills. Historically, and in common with most other northern towns, weaving was mainly the domain of women. In the first twenty years of the present century over half the working women in the town were engaged in either weaving or spinning, reflecting the importance of textiles to the local economy.

Above: More women, and one or two men, at work at the Tennyson Road Weaving Mill. The decline of Preston's weaving and spinning industry is well documented. From a peak of around 65 mills dedicated to textile weaving or cotton spinning at the time of the First World War, a combination of cheap foreign imports and outdated machinery resulted in fewer than ten mills remaining in operation in the 1980s and only two local textile companies actively engaged in this sector by the early 1990s.

Left and below, left: The Bond Motor Works at Ribbleton Lane, captured here in these two photographs from October 1965. In many ways the cars produced here were ahead of their time with their distinctive styling and lightweight fibreglass bodies. Triumph chassis and running gear should have completed a recipe for success, but it was not to be. There is still a strong appreciation and following for Bond cars of all types among enthusiasts all over the country, the six-cylinder high performance sports models being particular favourites. The three wheeled Bond cars were always seen as being in a head-to-head battle with their Reliant rivals and enjoyed a chequered pattern of success throughout their history, despite some interesting design features along the way.

Below: An evocative picture of a Dock Locomotive, three of which were kept at Preston shed and tasked with the job of supplying the Power Station with coal from the docks. The records show that in 1952 they were making twelve trips per day to the conveyor which fed the hungry furnaces.

Rotunda 1979

Rotunda 1981

Proposed Interior 1997

Then...
future...

now...

When St. George's Centre opened in 1966 it was at the forefront of a new generation of shopping centres.

Shoppers enjoyed the choice and convenience of a town centre shopping centre.

In 1981 the 'all under one roof' improvements were completed and shopping at St. George's became even better, come rain or shine!

At the beginning of 1997 work will commence on making St. George's bigger and better - with more shops, refurbished malls and entrances, improved security, better ventilation, new escalators and a lift.

It's all part of our objective - to keep St. George's and Preston at the forefront of shopping convenience.

ST. GEORGE'S CENTRE
Preston
Tel: 01772 204202

Street scenes remembered

Above and above, left: Two views of Lune Street in the 1950s.

Left: This photograph shows Marsh Lane and the Marsh Lane railway bridge as it was in 1980.

Above: A typical suburban scene from September 1959. The photograph shows the shopping parade on the Brookfield Estate. The business in the foreground is that operated by J & J Dilworth.

Above, right: Traffic jams on the London Road are nothing new. Here we see queues of traffic on one summer's afternoon in the late 1950s.

Right: Lancaster Road, south of Lord Street in 1964. Buildings as far along as Ribble Motor Services were demolished in order to make room for the building of the Guildhall.

Above: The Fylde Street roundabout with road improvements under way and the popular Lamb and Packet public house in the centre of the scene.

Above, right: This dramatic picture from October 1960 shows scaffolding in place during the construction of the Avenham Flats.

Right: An unusual view of Corporation Street and Fishergate, complete with point duty policeman.

Above: Many memories will be rekindled by this photograph of Gardner Street. The exact date when the picture was taken is not known, but estimated to be in the late 1940s or early 1950s.

Above, left: Ribble Buses were known in Preston and beyond. This picture shows the Ribble Booking Office in 1967.

Left: The Grand Junction roundabout seen here in August 1953, looking towards Maudland Works and Mills. Watery Lane is the road on the bottom left, Tulketh Road top left, and Water Lane top right.

To anyone who is not familiar with Preston the inclusion of this picture in a collection of nostalgic scenes may be a mystery. The Penwortham by-pass was a subject of much contention, and this view looking into Preston was described as "one of the most attractive approaches to a town I have ever seen" by a well known publisher of town guides. What a pity then that these magnificent trees had to be felled to make way for the road improvements.

Right: This view of Fishergate was captured about 1950. The most notable feature can be seen on the right - the remains of the Town Hall which had been destroyed by fire in 1947. This final reminder of the popular old building survived for another 12 years, until it was cleared in 1962.

Below: Not quite a 'now' picture, but near enough to make an interesting comparison. This photograph was taken some 30 years after the one above (approx. 1980) from virtually the same standpoint and by the same photographer, Peter G. Reed of Penwortham.

Fishergate - then and now

SHOPPING CENTRE

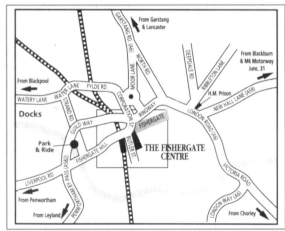

Fishergate's rising star of the retail world.....

Preston's shopping facilities were given a tremendous boost in the mid 1980s when the Fishergate Shopping Centre was built. One of the first stores to open there was Debenhams, and that was very quickly followed by many other leading retailers at this popular location, just yards away from the centre of the town and Preston's main line railway station.

Unlike some shopping centres in other towns,

Fishergate combines the best of both worlds; a very convenient location - with 850 car parking spaces and the railway station within easy reach - plus big store names and virtually everything the shopper needs all under one roof.

Unrivalled facilities

The Fishergate Shopping Centre has all the modern facilities demanded by today's shopper including excellent access, lifts and escalators capable of meeting the needs of the disabled visitor. All these are supported by additional features - ranging from a handy cash point machine to a convenient seating area which are certain to ensure the Centre's popularity with it's customers through to the next millenium.

Innovation

Retailers and Centre Management at Fishergate appreciate that their continued success relies upon much more than bricks and mortar - and consequently much emphasis is placed on the traditional values of quality and service. Throughout the year a full programme of promotional activity ensures that there is always something interesting to see and do at the Fishergate Shopping Centre. Innovative schemes have been put into place to heighten safety awareness and assist the visually handicapped. The centre may be a relative newcomer to the Preston retailing scene - but it is already a leader.

Be Aware Be Prepared!

Left: Mr Panda, the Fishergate Shopping Centre's mascot, and the "Be Aware", "Be Prepared" safety campaign.

1916 - 1996

Refrigeration pioneers celebrate 80 years in Preston

In 1916 a group of Preston butchers got together to form a cold store to provide themselves with week-end storage for meat and allow increased stocks to be held. At that time, the storage area was situated underneath Miller Arcade, the Victorian shopping arcade which had been built some twenty years earlier, right at the heart of retailing activity in Preston. The store moved across the road into premises at Glover's Court when the company was incorporated as Preston Cold Storage & Ice Co. in 1924.

Historic Connections

Preston Cold Store Ltd. is still owned by the descendants of those Edwardian butchers and the Board of Directors retains similar family connections. Until his death five years ago, Fred Hayes was the Chairman. His father, John had been a director and founder member. Fred was a well known refrigeration engineer, running his business for many years from premises in Hartington Road. Jack Bainbridge, who retired as a director in 1994, was brought up in his father's butchery business in Ribbleton Lane. His father, Arthur was also one of the founder members. Jack's tales from his childhood include carrying a bucket of blood across Preston on the bus (the conductor insisted that he stay on the platform at the back) and delivering beef quarters or full lamb carcasses on a bone shaking delivery boy's bike with hob nail boots as the main braking system. One of the current directors is Tim Rainford, who's grandfather 'T.C. Snr.' was a founder member. Tim's father 'T.C. Jnr.' and uncles were well known butchers at various locations in Preston and Blackpool. Colin Foster, Chartered Accountant and current Chairman has been connected with the company for many years as was his father before him. Colin's daughter, Jill who runs Foster & Co. (Chartered Accountants) continues the tradition. Bert Maddock was manager when the firm was located in Glover's Court and his son, Terry (the current managing director) remembers those premises from when he was a schoolboy at the nearby Catholic College. " The entrance to the yard consisted of a massive green folding gate with brickwork over the top. Some of the higher wagons would come in heavily laden and just fit under the arch. But when they had been off loaded and wanted to leave, they would have to let down their tyres to fit below the gate. The huge vehicle would then have to park, almost blocking Glover's Court whilst the driver struggled with a foot pump to re-inflate the tyres."

War Service

Such problems were thankfully left well behind when the company relocated in 1969 to the current site at Cromwell Road, Ribbleton on the outskirts of the Borough. Here, the war time Ministry food store was part of a network of similar facilities established throughout the country, all linked by rail to minimise wastage of Britain's precious food stocks. When the premises were built in 1941 the site was out in the country, surrounded by fields, agricultural holdings and a small railway station. Now surrounded by

quality housing, the directors and staff do their best to minimise any disturbance to the peace and serenity of this leafy suburb.

Expert Team

The company greatly values its decades of experience and technical expertise. "From the firm's beginnings right up to the present day, there has been a continuity of staff and directors. Knowledge and skills have been passed on and added to with each generation. However, our primary concern today is just as it was back in 1916: "customer satisfaction."

PRESTON COLD STORE LTD.
1916 - 1996

As one of the longest established cold storage facilities in the United Kingdom, Preston Cold Store Ltd has an enviable reputation for customer service and high standards of technical expertise. Conveniently situated within minutes of the M6 and M55 we are well placed, in every sense, to support the needs of a modern, high speed distribution network. We offer competitive rates for Frozen and Chill storage on a pallet or Tonne basis, as well as for depot rental.
Please telephone for further details.

PRESTON COLD STORE

UNITS TO LET
Cold rooms, offices, and process rooms available. Small and large units to suit your requirements. Rental covers maintenance of Plant, Buildings, Yards, Bays, Site Security and Lighting. Short and Long Term Lets

Members of the Cold Storage and Distribution Federation

Unit 2a
Ashworths Food Ltd.

Manufacturers of Quality Pies
213 Havelock Street, Preston.

Unit 13
NJM Bacon

Wholesale suppliers of sliced bacon

Telephone Preston 652371

Units 14 and 21
Kerfoots Traditional Foods

Tea Cakes, Batons, Savouries, Pies and Cakes.
Telephone Preston 702199

Unit 1
Mastercook Ltd

Food at its best - and home delivery of frozen food.
Telephone Preston 705440

Unit 18
Cottam Produce

Prepared Vegetable Supplies to caterers

Telephone Preston 793988

PRESTON COLD STORE LTD., CROMWELL ROAD, RIBBLETON, PRESTON, PR2 6YD   TEL: 01772 796117

Left: Drama indeed. Firemen cling on to the top of their turntable ladders at the height of the blaze in 1947 which claimed one of the best-loved buildings in Preston.

Below: Smouldering embers and charred timber were all that remained of the splendid building the day after the fire.

Town Hall Fire

Town Hall

Victory Parade

Left: The Town Hall, probably not long after its construction in 1867, in view of the absence of grime which was to blacken its fine Longridge stone walls over its all-too-short 80 year life. The building had taken five years to complete and was designed by Sir George Gilbert Scott.

Below: Crowds turned out throughout the land for victory parades some 50 years ago, and Preston was no exception. This photograph gives a good view of one of the most pleasing features of the building, the beautifully crafted open arches for which it was well known.

This photograph really captures a point in history, with all the atmosphere and pomp of a late nineteenth century Royal occasion. The scene is set in Cheapside, outside the Town Hall, in July 1885. Seen here is the escort assembled to honour the Prince of Wales - later Edward VII - on his visit to Preston.

Left: Miller Park took its name from Alderman Miller who purchased the 11 acres of land in 1864 and presented it to the town to create a public park. This form of philanthropy was quite typical of the age and would have been mirrored in similar towns throughout the land.

Below: Preston's Cenotaph, seen here in July 1962.

Above: The Harp Inn, Church Street, pictured here in February 1961.

Above, right: The Market Inn, on the corner of Lowthian Street and Market Street, in this photograph taken in May 1959.

Right: The Theatre Hotel in Fishergate, as it was in 1960.

Opposite page:

Top, right: Regatta Hotel, Fishergate Hill, which was pulled down for the new bridge approach in 1914. W.Allsop's shipyard machinery can be seen in the background of the picture.

Top, left: The popular "Old Dog" - where, in a room above, Martha Thomson started the first Methodist meetings.

Below, right: The Apollo Inn, Walker Street, in this picture which is thought to date from the mid 1950s.

*Favourite **Preston** watering holes...*

The Harris Museum and Art Gallery.

The Harris Museum and Art Gallery sits in the centre of Preston, dominating Market Square. It celebrated its centenary in 1993 and is the source of much pride to local people.

The Museum and Gallery is the result of a bequest from local lawyer Edmund Robert Harris who left £300,000 to the town in 1877 in memory of his father

the Rev. Robert Harris, Vicar of St George's. The sum was split equally to build the Harris Museum, the Harris Institute, and the Harris Orphanage. The period was one of local philanthropy with business and clergy across the country forming a movement to bring culture to the "lower classes".

The architect of the building was James Hibbert who used the Greek Revival style to portray the high cultural standards reached by the Ancient Greeks whom he wished to emulate. The foundation stone was laid in 1882 as part of the Guild Celebrations by the Duke of Lathom. Improvements to the town centre took place at the same time to show the Harris building off to its full advantage.

Preston already had significant museum collections based in the Literary and Philosophical Society in Cross Street before the Harris was founded. The Harris Trustees provided funds of £15,000 to purchase new exhibits covering geology, natural history, archaeology, numismatics and the visual arts.

The collections have been added to over the years with significant bequests including the Newsham art collection, Houghton ceramics and the Mrs French

collection of scent bottles and visiting card cases. Membership of the Contemporary Art Society has ensured that the Harris has continued to collect more avant-garde paintings and sculpture and formed a distinctive collection of British art from the 1980s and 1990s.

Today's Harris building has seen a number of changes since its foundation last century. The covered entrance has been enclosed and a commission by artist Ian Hamilton Finlay now dominates the area.

Mezzanine floors and a costume gallery have been added to increase the area available and improvements made to the environmental conditions in the galleries. The magnificent Egyptian balcony, featuring murals by John Somerscales, has had a face-lift and remains a popular trip for visitors with regular organised tours.

The collections are now based around social history, fine and decorative art. An innovative exhibitions programme stages over 12 temporary exhibitions each year ensuring that the frequent visitor will enjoy something new on each visit. Education and interpretation is an integral part of the work with workshops and activities arranged for every exhibition for the young and old alike.

The Harris has won acclaim in many areas of its operation. It was the only provincial gallery to be included in the Observer's Top Ten exhibitions for 1994, was quoted by the Arts Council as promoting good practice in its disabled access, and voted 'Museum of Year' by local people in "Lancashire Life" in 1993.

Facing page, bottom left: 'Head of a Bride' modelled by R. Monti for Copeland, 1861.
Facing page, top right: The Harris Building c.1900.
Above left: 'Dorette' by Gerald Leslie Brockhurst, 1933.

Top: 'The Resurrection' by Stanley Spencer, 1946
Above: Pieces from the Mrs French Collection of scent bottles

They don't build them like this anymore.

Within this splendidly refurbished Victorian Arcade you will find speciality shops providing a wide range of high quality goods and services. In July 1996 the Miller Arcade proudly celebrated its centenary, and the Grade II listed building remains as beautiful as it did when it was first opened, thanks to a continuous programme of maintenance undertaken by specialist craftsmen. Few shopping arcades in Great Britain can compare with the breathtaking Victorian splendour which has long been associated with the Miller Arcade - a fact that the citizens of Preston can be proud of. Modern day shoppers may browse around the wide variety of shops at their leisure, in the unique atmosphere of peace and quiet created by the elegant Victorian surroundings.

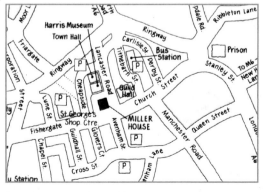

1896 - 1996

MILLER ARCADE
CHURCH STREET, PRESTON, LANCASHIRE.

The Miller Arcade: a special place in the affections of Preston folk for 100 years.

In 1895 following a visit to New York, Mr Nathaniel Miller, a Preston Dentist, held a competition for the design of a "fireproof arcade" for his large town centre island site. 20 entries were received, with the winner being of "Spanish Renaissance style. The design included shops, a wine lodge, an hotel and offices, and borrowed features from earlier Continental developments such as the Galleria Vittoria Emanuele II in Milan, the Galleria Umberto in Naples and El Tergesteo in Trieste.

Miller house was opened in 1901 to great public acclaim. The cosmopolitan and innovative design was particularly exciting in what was then an ordinary northern mill town. The ornate and elegant elevations clad in buff and brown terracotta tiles with motifs of foliage, flowers and fruit introduced in a style not previously seen in Preston.

Glazed roof

The central arcade with barrel-vaulted glazed roof supported by pierced and decorated cast-iron arches, and with a patterned tiled floor, became the popular hub of the Town Centre. Many people in the Preston area will recall the time when the arcade was a popular meeting place for couples about to set out for a night out - and the many years when the arcade served as the terminus for trams and buses.

Many well known retailers have had outlets in the arcade over the years - familiar names include Whittles Jewellers, The Gift house, Smirk's Sweets,

Dunns outfitters and Sharpes Fashions. At one time, in the days before refrigerators, the cellars in the arcade were used as a cold store for meat by the butchers in the town. Turkish Baths, the King's Arms public house and the Crown Hotel were other popular features of the Miller Arcade. Shortly after the Second World War, ownership of the Miller Arcade passed to a Yorkshire company which renamed it *Arndale House*. Perhaps predictably, local people would have none of this - and continued to refer to the precinct as the Miller Arcade. When

the new bus station was constructed in 1969 the arcade suffered a substantial loss in trade.

Rejuvenation and renewal

Three years later, however, the building was the subject of a restoration programme leading to the reopening of the facility - much to the relief of local people. In 1985, a total restoration costing half a million pounds was successfully completed, returning the Miller Arcade to its original splendour. Today, visitors from all over the U.K and beyond are drawn to the jewel in the crown of Preston retailing.

footballing favourites....

Above: Tom Finney, always known for his ability to steal an extra yard on his opponents, in a characteristic shot from October 1959. The match seen here was Blackburn Rovers versus Preston North End at Ewood Park - watched by an enthusiastic crowd of 41,000. The goal being scored here by Finney was one of the four scored by his team which beat the Rovers by four goals to one. This marvellous picture was taken by Howard Talbot from Blackburn.

Above, right: Celebrations in full flow on a damp afternoon in 1954 after Preston North End return from Wembley in 1954. "Celebrations" may not have been the right word - they had lost 2 - 3 to West Bromwich Albion in the Cup Final.

Right: A rather sheepish Alan Ball was the centre of attention in this scene depicting the celebrations when Preston North End won the third division trophy in May 1971.

Star team...what price now?

Above: A remarkable photograph - supplied by Howard Talbot of Blackburn - and showing the famous footballing heroes gathered at Preston for the Tom Finney benefit match on 26 September 1960. The Tom Finney 11 versus the All Stars 11. Just look at the players - back row, left to right, Jimmy Armfield (England and Blackpool), Nat Lofthouse (England and Bolton), Alex Parker (Scotland and Everton), Bert Trautman (Manchester City), Wilf Mannion (England and Middlesborough), Billy Liddle (Scotland and Liverpool), Bill Shankly (Scotland and Preston), Seated: Stanley Matthews (England, Blackpool and Stoke), Stanley Mortenson (England and Blackpool), Tom Finney (host) England and Preston, Neil Franklin (England and Stoke), Billy Wright (England and Wolves). What a team - how much would they be worth now!
Left: Preston North End returning home after having lost 2-3 to West Ham in the 1964 Cup Final.
Above, left: Nobby Stiles leads the celebrations in May 1978 after the club won promotion.

The story of Ashworth Foods Ltd

The story behind the successful Preston food manufacturer, Ashworths Foods Ltd, is as intriguing as any involving a family business which has earned success through determination, enterprise and liberal helpings of true northern grit.

The company was founded in 1950 by Mr and Mrs Norman Ashworth in buildings attached to their home at Havelock Street. Initially the manufacture of cooked meats, sausages, black puddings and polony was for a meat-starved public after the Second World War. Later, customers knowing Mrs Ida Ashworth's particular gift for baking, asked her to make a few pies, and soon her reputation spread throughout the area. Other retailers began selling the pies and cooked meat products - and the basis for the

Mrs Ida Ashworth in the street where it all began.

Above: Norman Ashworth outside his butchers shop.
Below, right: A 1978 picture showing the delivery fleet.

business as we know it today began to take shape.

Deliveries

In 1955 the Ashworth's son, Peter joined the growing family business. Peter would help make the pies and cooked meats as well as deliver them to an ever expanding network of retail outlets. Soon it was necessary to buy a second van to meet the demand, and soon after that the Ashworth's first extension was built. The year was 1956.

Further expansion

In 1963 Mrs Kathleen Kennedy joined her parents and brother in the family business. Mrs Peter Ashworth joined the company in 1964 following the birth of their sons John and Brian. Initially Mrs Ashworth helped make the increasing number of deliveries - but later, as the company's administrative burden grew, she took over the running of the busy office.

After the death of Mr Norman Ashworth, the co-founder, Peter and Kathleen became partners with Mrs Ida Ashworth, to carry the business into the second half of the century. The demand for Ashworth's products continued to grow as their reputation spread further. Rapid expansion followed; two vans became four - then six, and in 1979 a further extension was built. John Ashworth and David Kennedy, Kathleen's son, joined the company, and they were soon followed by Brian Ashworth and Susan Kennedy, Kathleen's daughter.

Expansion in the 1980s

Redevelopment of the area around Havelock Street was on the cards in the early 1980s. The family decided that this was the ideal time to expand their own premises if they were not to be left behind. They must have wondered what they were letting themselves in for, as the whole of the management team became preoccupied with the prospect of even more

building work and expansion, and the next few years were to tax everyone's patience and good humour with the many planning and construction challenges they were to face. At the end of all the heartache and uncertainty the family was able to extend the factory on the present site. With the development of

1980s construction underway.

Preston New Town, Havelock Street, as it had been known altered beyond all recognition. It was a turbulent time for people in the neighbourhood, and the Ashworth family shared this emotional roller coaster ride along with local residents.

Despite the greatly enlarged facilities, the company had to expand further in 1986, and purchased land around Bold Street. Even more expansion took place towards the end of the decade to accommodate a large freezer section for this new product range.

Quality and service

The demand for the company's products had grown consistently on the back of their reputation for fine quality and the highest standards of hygiene and customer service. New technology and new product lines have been two key elements in the success story

that is *Ashworth Foods.* Throughout the company there is a sense of pride in the products which are produced by the local workforce and dispatched to towns and cities throughout the country. Now, as in the 1950s when Ida Ashworth first started baking her pies, no effort is spared to make sure that every pie is the *best* they can produce. Success has definitely not changed the character or company ethos at Ashworth's; family members retain a very hands-on involvement with all aspects of the production, distribution and management of the firm. Emphasis is placed on keeping close to the workforce and in-tune with the needs of the customer - in the same way that Norman and Ida first did.

And into the present...

As the Ashworth reputation for good quality pies, pasties and sausage rolls grew, enquiries came from

Members of the distribution team in 1989

further afield, hence the decision to exhibit at the national exhibition "Bake '93". Following this, Ashworth's products are now being sold in all parts of the U.K, from the Highlands of Scotland down to the Channel Islands. Enquiries also came from abroad, and in March 1994 the first shipment left for Majorca. An exhibition in Barcelona in March 1996 paved the way for further export orders, and Ashworth's products are now sold in Denmark, Spain and the Canary Islands.

Very few companies in the whole of the U.K can claim to have achieved the impressive growth that is evident at Ashworths Foods Ltd. For all that success the company still behaves in the way that the family business did in it's earliest days - striving for ways of making better products and finding new ways of creating highly satisfied customers - just as Norman and Ida Ashworth did in the 1950s.

Expansion on the way at St. George's Shopping Centre.

St. George's Shopping Centre is right in the heart of Preston town centre and has everything you need, all under one roof. There is a superb selection of shops with the widest possible choice of goods, several meeting places where you can relax over lunch or have a quick cup of tea and an excellent rotunda for promotions and community events.

Come rain or shine you are assured of friendly service and value for money at each of the outlets within the Centre whilst security guards keep a low profile and solve any problems as they arise. Since the installation of a a sophisticated security system parents and children are safe to shop with peace of mind.

The Centre has its own 450 space multi storey car park which recently won a gold award for being a safe and secure car park, the first of its kind in the North West. There are disabled toilet facilities on the top floor along with baby changing room, public telephones, public toilets and the car park entrance. The Management Office is also found here and there is someone available at all times to deal with any queries from the general public.

St. George's Centre, which is owned by Legal and General, was opened 30 years ago on March 22 1966 as a non-covered Shopping Centre. In 1981 the Centre was substantially refurbished and also received a roof, together with environmental control systems, this being the first occasion an exercise of this type was undertaken on a working shopping centre in the U.K. It is arranged on three levels, providing 250,000 sq.ft of retailing space and comprises 113 retail units and a multi storey car park of 450 spaces.

The Centre is anchored by W.H. Smiths, Mothercare, Marks and Spencer, Superdrug, Adams Childrenswear, Dorothy Perkins and Vision Express. In 1997 work will commence to provide 117,000 sq.ft of retail space by constructing 30 new units and three refurbished units fronting Friargate. The net additional retail floor space will be approximately 25,000 sq.ft giving the scheme a new retail floor space of 275,000 sq. ft. The redevelopment is to be done in three phases and the works are scheduled to take approximately two and a half years. The estimated cost is some £23 million.

Family-operated Spar chain celebrates 50 years service in the region.

Preston's family run chain of Spar stores celebrated its fiftieth anniversary in 1996. The business was founded in 1946 at Walmer Bridge by Mr and Mrs Jack Hunt. From its modest beginnings, the company has grown consistently over the years and now operates 21 Spar stores from Lancaster to Bolton and Wigan to Morecambe.

The founders son - Lawrence Hunt - became involved in the business in 1950 - and is the only one of Jack Hunt's children to have followed him into the family firm. Lawrence started at the bottom, working initially as a shop assistant to get a thorough grounding in the business before moving up to store management. A significant milestone in the development of the store chain was the decision to join the Spar organisation in 1957.

"Spar" was established in Holland and now operates in 25 countries all over the world. In 1960 a second store was acquired - in Longton, followed seven years later by a third at Lostock Hall. Lawrence Hunt bought the business from his father when he retired in 1969.

Rapid growth

Under the stewardship of Lawrence Hunt the company has experienced rapid growth and further success. On average, a new store has been opened every year since 1969 - a remarkable achievement. Another important milestone in the development of the firm was the advent of the "Eight 'Till Late" concept. This offered customers the greater convenience of longer shopping hours with no half day or lunchtime closing - along with the convenience that Sunday opening brings. The

family business element of the company is assured now that two of Lawrence Hunt's three children have joined him in the firm; daughter Jill joined in 1980 after gaining valuable experience in the wholesale side of the operation, and was followed by her brother Kevin some eight years later who had had the benefit of having gained valuable experience with a family operating a Spar outlet in Austria. Lawrence Hunt is proud of the role that his family firm now plays in the community; "We employ more than 300 people, 10 of whom have worked for us for more than 20 years - and 30 others for more than 10 years". "We like to think that we have an approach to business which combines the virtues of the past with the advantages of the present" says Mr Hunt.

Friargate - as we know it today

A family firm since 1909

Friargate - as it was at the turn of the century

Bambers of Preston - a family tradition

In the fast moving world of modern town centre retailing some stores seem to switch sites so often, its a wonder they don't put their stock, staff and fittings on castors! The paint barely seems to dry on one shopping centre before they're laying foundations for the next. And as soon as the ground is broken, the multiples are queueing up for space, convinced that each new complex will be bigger, brighter and a better crowd puller than the last.

All this high blood pressure stuff, however, is not really the style of Richard Bamber & Son Limited of Preston. The town has its share of smart shopping developments, but this particular cabinet and upholstery specialist has never been interested in applying for space. In fact, it has only moved once in 87 years - and that was only a couple of hundred yards.

The present store is situated at the lower end of Friargate, near to the University of Central Lancashire roundabouts.

"We like it here. It suits us and it suits the furniture we carry" says Donald Bamber who runs the business with his brother Richard. And, as it's a more relaxing place to shop than the hectic town centre, they maintain, it also suits their customers. The intriguing layout of the store, he says, results from the fact that it is actually four knocked into one. It was built up bit by bit by the Bamber brothers' father Harry, and grandfather

The present-day staff pose for a picture at Bambers.

Bambers friendly and helpful delivery team

Richard, after the war. At the time, they ran a flourishing second-hand and antique furniture business which Richard Bamber had started some 40 years earlier.

"The first site had just become too small and the first part of the shop in Friargate became available" says Mr Bamber. "Later they picked up the other three, which included a tailors and a tripe shop. We also bought the old mill behind the yard and a couple of cottages out at the back which we knocked down to improve access. When the piecemeal purchase was complete, the Bambers had created a single store covering 12,000 sq. ft., over two floors. But, while the partition walls have been removed from the main entrance area, there are lots of nooks and crannies, and upstairs almost separate rooms, complete with chimney breasts and fireplaces. It is the ideal backdrop for room settings , and, say the Bambers, more inter-

esting for customers to browse around than a modern open plan store.

Once in its new premises, the business developed and expanded. Richard junior joined his father and grandfather - sadly now both deceased - after being articled to an auctioneer, and Donald went to work in the shop straight from school. As time went on the store also gradually changed direction, moving into top quality furniture and away from the antiques market. "It was partly a natural development and partly because of the scarcity of good pieces" says Mr Bamber. Other members of the Bamber family involved in the business are Donald's wife Dorothy, daughters Gillian and Susan, and Richard's wife Jean, daughter Sara and son-in-law David. As one recent customer said "I thought I had died and gone to heaven - I have never seen so much beautiful furniture under one roof before".

R. Slinger & Son - the Preston family ironmongers now in it's sixth generation.

In 1858, Richard Slinger started the firm of iron-mongers and woodworking machine suppliers in the heart of Preston at Maudland Bank. Over the years the firm has occupied several different premises in the town centre, the first move being to 165 Friargate in 1875. This was the age of major industrial devel-opment, and Richard Slinger was quick to exploit the many opportunities that this presented for his grow-ing company. A particular specialism was wood-working machinery. In the early days, before the advent of electric power, the customers who bought them would use line shafts and belts to transmit the energy from steam engines in the mills and factories which were springing up in the area. The company's expertise and reputation grew and *Slingers* were soon delivering machines to firms throughout the north west.

William James Slinger followed his father into the business at around the time of the move to Friargate. This coincided with the decision to carry a broader range of ironmongery items - as well as goods of a

An atmospheric early view of Slingers Friargate store

more domestic nature, such as cooking ranges, fire-places, garden tools and cooking utensils.

The move to Corporation Street

In 1902 the company acquired large premises in Corporation Street in addition to the Friargate store, and retained them until 1970. This enabled the com-pany to display the range of fireplaces, kitchen ranges and plumbing equipment in more spacious surroundings. Isaac Richard Slinger was the grand-

father of the present chairman and managing direc-tor, Mr Richard William Slinger, and, at the time of his death in 1965, had been associated with the com-pany for 68 years. Employees at R. Slinger & Son remember how Isaac Richard Slinger would recount tales of him cycling around the Lake District seeking new customers for his range of woodworking machinery over 80 years ago. Orders would then be delivered by rail, and later road transport. In the early days horses and carts had been the norm!

A milestone in the development of the firm was it's

Above: The company celebrated it's centenary by holding a dinner for the staff and their partners at the Windemere Hydro Hotel in September 1958. A youthful Richard Slinger is seated third from the left.

Left: The familiar shop on Friargate in the 1950s. ***Right:*** An advert from 1915.

R. SLINGER & SON,
FURNISHING & BUILDERS' IRONMONGERS,
TOOL DEALERS & CUTLERS.
TELEGRAMS— TELEPHONE—
"SLINGER, PRESTON." No. 335 (2 Lines).
MERCHANTS and
MANUFACTURERS.
MILL FURNISHERS.
RANGE
MANUFACTURERS
Friargate & Corporation Street, PRESTON.

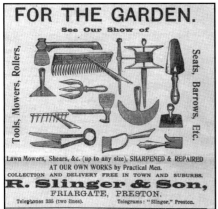

FOR THE GARDEN.
See Our Show of

Tools, Mowers, Rollers,   Seats, Barrows, Etc.

Lawn Mowers, Shears, &c. (up to any size), SHARPENED & REPAIRED AT OUR OWN WORKS by Practical Men.
COLLECTION AND DELIVERY FREE IN TOWN AND SUBURBS.
R. Slinger & Son,
FRIARGATE, PRESTON.
Telephones 335 (two lines).   Telegrams: "Slinger," Preston.

Left: An advertisement from 1910. *Below, left:* The spacious *Slingers* store on Corporation Street.

appointment as dealers and agents for the Aga Cooker company in 1937. The company remains one of the few dealers in the region for these exclusive products. Many Preston folk will remember the 1964 move from the Orchard Street premises to Lune Street. The business operated this outlet for 16 years, until its closure in 1980. In 1990, the father of the current MD, Mr Richard Slinger, retired after achieving

a staggering 63 years service with the company.

Move to Paley Road
In 1970, R. Slinger & Son moved to it's present location in Paley Road. This was mainly because of the growing need of the business to be accessible to large lorries making their deliveries - as well as making it easier for customers to park.

Proud of their family roots..
The firm is proud to have been owned and managed by the same family since the start. The latest member to join the firm is Peter Richard Slinger - in 1990, his aunt, Susan Joan Caunce has been working with his father there since 1957. Throughout the firm, staff are proud of it's long history, but this does not mean that they spend all their time looking back. "We like to think that our customers feel we successfully combine all the advantages of the present with the virtues of the past" says current Chairman and MD Richard Slinger. The first Richard Slinger would have been proud.

R. Baron Ltd - Preston craftsmen for almost a century

Few Preston people will be aware of the wealth of history that lies behind the joinery company known as R. Baron Ltd. The exact date that the company was founded is unknown, but it was *incorporated* - becoming a limited company - in 1918. Robert Baron, began carrying out domestic repairs and coffin making around the Deepdale area of Preston in the earliest days of the company, walking 4 or 5 miles to each job and returning to his workshop for lunch each day! Obviously very few businesses had the benefit of motorised transport in those days - and Robert would use a handcart to transport his tools and materials through the cobbled streets to each job.

Peel Hall Street Works

At around the time of the start of the First World War the move was made to Peel Hall Street -the location of the company today. Robert Baron continued to run the business himself until the end of the Second World War, when responsibility passed to his two sons, William Albert Baron and Robert Roland Baron - the father of the current managing director, Robert John Baron.

Right from the early days, training was always considered to be an essential ingredient of the company's success - a belief that has literally been handed down from generation to generation. The founder of the firm was virtually self-taught, and this is perhaps why he insisted that his sons received the best training in their craft available - at the Harris Technical College.

Developments at the Peel Hall Street works included the construction of a purpose built workshop and timber yard, later extended to a two-storey workshop to accommodate the growth that the company was experiencing. This growth was connected with the firm's concentration on two key areas - maintenance and retail shop fitting.

In the years after the Second World War a more sophisticated approach to retailing and the retail shop environment resulted in a growing demand for shop fitting services and *Barons* took advantage of the trend. The company's ability to work closely with retail customers and produce top quality work for them was to prove central to it's survival and eventual success.

Turning point

In 1951 the company received a telephone call from the manager of a large retailer - the job, repairing a broken rainwater pipe, was small but urgent. The request was attended to quickly and efficiently, and it was to be the start of a close relationship with one of the firm's most valued customers - Marks and Spencer plc. What makes this story all the more memorable is that the plumber who was sent out on

Left: This amusing cartoon was drawn by Bill Baron in the 1950s and it depicts his tongue-in-cheek impression of how some customers think a busy builders office operates: "Rows of tradesmen waiting on their hooks for the telephone to ring... a greasy pole to allow them to get to the van waiting outside with it's engine running"

utilities, several banks and government departments, and many High Street stores.

The present day

The current managing director of R. Baron Ltd, Robert John Baron, has firm views about the reasons for the company's success over the years and prospects for continued growth. "Our customers appreciate the value of dealing with a company which is managed with traditional "family business values" very much in mind. The thing to remember is that only happy customers come back; over the years everyone in the firm has worked hard to please our customers - no matter how big or small the job involved - and I judge our success by the level of repeat business we have achieved. One of our strengths is the fact that all the current directors are family members. With a staff of 15 we are able to stay very close to our customers and to keep abreast of their changing needs". Training continues to be a major strength and it is no coincidence that several of the staff who joined the firm as apprentices have stayed on until retirement. "It is that kind of continuity and commitment that

this crucial assignment was no less than the soon-to-be-famous footballer Tom Finney! The local *Marks and Spencer* relationship flourished as the respected retail organisation began to appreciate the quality of workmanship and the ability *Barons* have to liaise closely with their clients. It was not long before the company was appointed regional contractor for Marks and Spencer plc with responsibility for maintaining seventeen major stores in the region, with a watching brief at a further fourteen stores.

Other milestones in the development of the firm have included the fitting out of the first Kentucky Fried Chicken restaurant in the U.K - in Preston of course - as well as many other well known organisations, including Preston North End Football Club, public

retains as well as attracts our best customers" says Robert Baron an opinion, no doubt, that his grandfather would have agreed with.

Pictured above: A team of joiners pause for a rare photograph at the turn of the century.
Above, left: Tom Finney, of football fame, but seen here discussing building and plumbing, with Bill Baron and Cyril Naylor, a former manager of Marks and Spencer plc, Preston.

YOUR LOCAL NEIGHBOURHOOD STORE

"For Your Everyday Needs"

Best for local shopping

For further information about James Hall & Company (Southport) Ltd
please telephone us on 01772 706666 or write to:
SPAR Distribution Centre 89 - 91 Blackpool Road, Ribbleton, Preston, Lancs PR2 6DY

School days

Left: This is picture of St. Paul's school, which was taken in March 1965 will evoke strong memories from former pupils.

Right: St. Thomas's school and a class of five or six-year-olds with their stern looking teacher and a selection of favourite china dolls in 1918.

Left: A book about the Preston area would surely not be complete without a picture of Arkwright Hall which was built in 1728 and restored in 1980. This picture was taken in 1946. Arkwright invented the *water-frame* here in 1768.

Right: Stoneygate, one of the town's oldest thoroughfares, as it was in 1936.

Top: A charming scene from 1904 - Moor Park.